Java Programming:
Beginning Beginners' Guide

By

Keshav Patel

LearnToProgram Media

Vernon, Connecticut

LearnToProgram.tv, Incorporated
27 Hartford Turnpike Suite 206
Vernon, CT 06066

contact@learntoprogram.tv

(860) 840-7090

ISBN-13: 978-0692614914
ISBN-10: 0692614915
©2015 by LearnToProgram.tv, Incorporated

About the Beginning Beginners' Guide Series

This Beginning Beginner's series of books was born out of a frustration: Most Beginning books on web and mobile development were not designed for true beginners.

Often in beginners' books the language was over complicated and laden with jargon that only those with programming experience understand. The books assume too much prior knowledge or experience. In the end, many people new to programming gnashed their teeth in frustration and gave up.

The fact is that programming is completely approachable and even fun to learn if taught correctly.

That's exactly what the Beginning Beginners' Guide series aims to do: Help true beginners learn to code.

This series of programming books is for you if you've never written a line of code before—or if you've tried to learn from other books unsuccessfully. You CAN learn to code well. You don't have to be mathematically oriented, or uber-intelligent.

Learning to code won't always be easy—but it is doable. If you can manipulate an Excel spreadsheet, you can learn programming.

Here's hoping that the process for you is as rewarding as it is for us to teach.

Should you have questions or comments, please email me directly at mark@learntoprogram.tv.

-Mark Lassoff, Founder
 LearnToProgram Media

TABLE OF CONTENTS

Chapter 1:
Writing Your First Program

Welcome. If this is your first time programming, congratulations! You're about to start an adventure that most find very rewarding. If you are trying to learn after a previous abortive attempt, you deserve recognition as well. Tackling programming isn't always easy—but it's not outside the grasp of the average person, either.

Over the years, I've taught programming to over 500,000 people both online and in person. The programmers I've met over the years—both beginners and seasoned vets—have come from a variety of backgrounds. I've found that both PhDs and high school dropouts can make good programmers. I've had mathematicians, psychiatrists, and 12 year-olds in my classes over the years and all have been able to learn some programming.

You will learn too. In this introductory chapter—which is specially designed for the slightly apprehensive beginner—I am going to take you step-by-step through the process of writing your first program. You don't need any special equipment except a laptop or desktop computer.

So without further delay, let's get started!

What You're Going to Learn
This first chapter will serve as an introduction on setting up your programming environment and getting started. Each chapter following is designed to take you through the basics of a certain aspect of

development and give you a foundation for greater learning. Just to give you some context, here's what's coming up in the rest of the book:

Chapter 2: Input and Output
Input and output are key to any program. In this chapter we'll look at how to get data into and out of a program.

Chapter 3: Understanding Variables
Variables are key building blocks in any program. This chapter takes readers through declaring and utilizing variables in expressions. Video tutorial included.

Chapter 4: Conditionals and Loops
Conditionals and Loops are structures which allow programs to make decisions that alter the execution of the program and result. These will be demonstrated and explained in this chapter.

Chapter 5: Dealing with Data
Almost every useful program, to some extent, deals with data. In this chapter you'll learn how to store various forms of data in a program.

Chapter 6: Putting it All Together
In this final chapter, readers will learn how to create a useful program that processes and stores data, using the skills developed in the previous chapters.

Before we write any programs, we have to get your development environment set up. I won't make you buy anything and you'll have a few options to choose from.

Figure 1.1: The Author's Development Environment. Doobie Brothers' music not included

Setting Up Your Development Environment

We're going to be using a language called Java in this book. Installing Java on your machine is rather simple and the process is generally the same for most major operating systems. With your browser you're going to want to navigate to oracle.com. Oracle is the company that maintains Java, and the JDK (Java Development Kit) that you need to download to write code in Java.

Once at Oracle.com, find "Downloads" on the top menu bar and click on "Java for Developers" under "Popular Downloads".

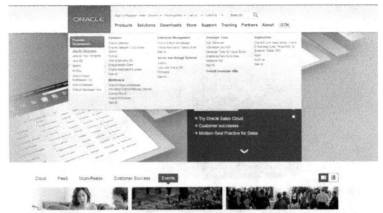

Figure 1.2: Oracle.com with the Downloads menu open.

After clicking that link you will see a download page. A dialog box will appear that reads JDK, with a download button under it. When you click it, it will redirect you to a page where you can select your operating system. The website will provide a set of instructions detailing how to go about installing the JDK onto your computer.

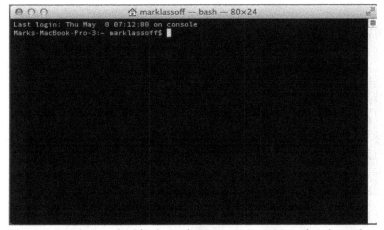

Figure 1.3: The terminal in the author's computer. Note that the author changed the default colors through the terminal's preferences

In the event that you'd rather not go through the process of installing a JDK to your machine I recommend you use the virtual Linux server provided by my friends at Koding.com. Point your browser to www.Koding.com and register for their free account. The free account gives you a virtual Linux machine that you can access through your web browser—and it can compile and run Java code right out of the box! No downloads are required. It's what I used to write the code we'll be using in this book.

Once you have your account, click the button to turn on your Virtual Machine(VM) and get coding. You'll be using a text editor on Koding to type Java files and the terminal to run them.

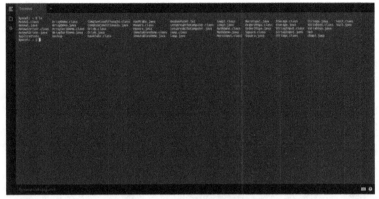

Figure 1.4: Command Line (or Terminal) in Koding.com.

Writing and Running Your Code

Now that you have your environment set up, it's time to (finally) write some code. We'll write code in a text editor. A text editor is different than a word processor. A word processor will introduce invisible formatting code into a file. If you were to run code written in a word processor it would likely cause an error due to the embedded formatting code.

A text editor, on the other hand, saves the text you enter as pure text—without introducing any unnecessary formatting. The text produced by a text editor can be easily processed by the Java compiler. Within the command line environments in the Koding.com virtual machine and on the Mac there are two text editors you can use. They are known as *nano* and *vi*. These text editors have a heritage that goes back to the 1970s—so as you use them you can truly feel "old school!"

The other option is to use the default text editor on Koding, TextEdit on a Mac or Notepad on Windows. They're all rather self-explanatory, although some may need a few settings changed to highlight Java code. As a side note, make sure that whenever you first save your code files, you save them as "filename.java".

nano

Nano is an easy to use Linux-based editor. It's pretty intuitive. You can simply start typing your code when the nano environment loads. Nano has a number of control codes which are listed at the bottom of your screen for your reference. The most important to note are CTRL-O which saves your file and CTRL-X which exits nano and returns you to the command line.

By default, nano will save your file in the same folder you were in when you opened nano itself.

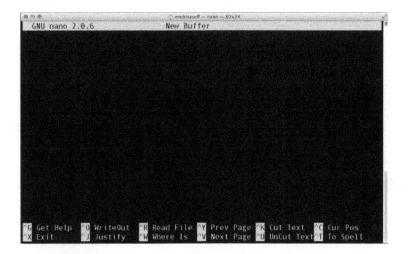

Figure 1.5: The nano text editor.

You can start nano by typing **nano** and then hit enter on the command line.

vi

vi is a slightly more complex (and even more "old school") text editor. The most important thing to understand about vi is that there are two modes: command mode and insert mode. To enter insert mode, press 'i' on your keyboard. When you want to move into command mode to issue commands like write and quit, hit the ESC key. If you screw up and find yourself in the wrong mode, press ESC a lot and that seems to get you back into command mode from wherever you are at.

There's an old joke about vi that goes like this: *vi has two modes, and you're in the wrong one.* (If you don't think that's funny right now, you will after you use vi for a bit!)

When you enter vi, type **i** to move into insert mode and you'll be able to type your code. When you're done, hit ESC to move into command mode. All commands must be preceded by a colon. So to write your file you'll enter **:w**. To quit you'll enter **:q**. vi also lets you combine commands. For example, the combination **:wq** will write your file and then quit back to the command line.

Figure 1.6: vi wants you to help poor children in Uganda. It offers limited help for new programmers worldwide.

You can start vi by typing **vi** and then hitting return on the command line.

So now you should have your text editor started and be ready to enter your code. Enter the following code into your text editor exactly as it appears:

```
public class HelloWorld{

    public static void main (String[] args) {

        System.out.println("This is my first program!");
        System.out.println("Programmers are rockstars!");
    }
}
```

It should be at least somewhat evident what this code does. The **println()** function prints content to the command line. In this case you are printing two strings. Strings are simply lines of characters. Strings are always enclosed in quotes.

Once you've typed the code, it's time to run it. In nano, save your file by typing CTRL-W. When prompted, enter the filename **HelloWorld.java**. The ".java" extension indicates that this is a Java source code file. Next enter CTRL-X to quit and you'll return to the command line. In vi, enter command mode and then save your file by typing **:w HelloWorld.java**. This writes your file under the appropriate file name. Finally, in vi, hit **:q** to quit and return to the command line. In any other editor, including the one on Koding, generally you can open a menu and click 'save as' just like you would in any other computer program.

Notice that the filename we gave this program matches the name of the class (HelloWorld). This is the Java standard. This standard makes class files easily identifiable in build when you have multiple source files. So for housekeeping purposes, whenever you make a new '.java' file make sure that the name of the class in the code (which is written after 'public class' in the first line of the code.) matches the name of the file. This way anyone reading your code will know which '.class' file is associated with what '.java' file.

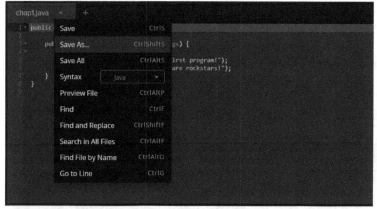

Figure 1.7: Saving your file in Koding.

Now that you have typed your code into an editor, open your terminal, and your cursor should appear at the prompt. Run the program by entering the following at the prompt (don't type the '$'—that just represents the prompt itself):

$ javac HelloWorld.java
$ java HelloWorld

The first line here commands Java to compile the source code that you wrote into what's known as Java byte code and write it to a '.class' file. This byte code is executed by the Java Virtual Machine (or JVM) whenever you run your program. JVMs can be installed on numerous devices, from cellphones to supercomputers, and they all do the same thing: run Java code. The result of this is Java's ability to run on multiple platforms. So long as a JVM is installed on a machine, it can run the compiled Java code that you write.

The second line instructs Java to actually run what's in the '.class' file. Note that the '.class' is implied. You don't have to type it when you run your code. If you open the folder where the file is saved, you will see it as a '.class' file though.

If you've done everything correctly you should see the result of your program printed before the next prompt.

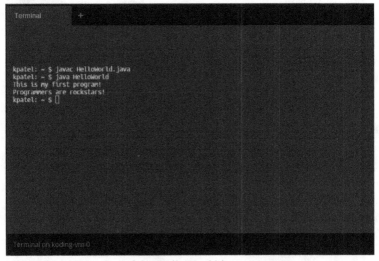

Figure 1.8: Execution of the HelloWorld.java program

If your output doesn't look similar to figure 1.9, you need to load your text editor and code again and find your error. You can reload your code at the command line prompt with the following command:

vi: **vi HelloWorld.java**
nano: **nano HelloWorld.java**

In any other editor, open the file as you would any other.

Some common errors include:
-Not closing brackets
-Forgetting semicolons at the end of lines
-Mistyping "public static void main(String[] args)" (It's case sensitive!)

Congratulations! You have successfully written your first program.

Understanding the println() function
In the preceding example we used the println function to output a string. The print function is also capable of printing out the following types of data:

Integers: Integers are "whole numbers" and don't have a decimal point. In Java, you can print an integer like this:

System.out.println(2573);

Floating Point Numbers: Floats are more precise numbers that include a decimal point. In Java you can print a floating point number like this:

System.out.println(3.45783);

Expressions: Expressions must be evaluated before a result is determined. Expressions are usually arithmetic problems. To print an expression in Java:

System.out.println(3.0/(6+4));

In the expression above, the part of the expression in parenthesis will be evaluated first due to the order of operations. The result printed is 0.3.

We'll look at expressions more closely in our next chapter.

As a side note, it's good to understand that the println function is a version of the **print()** function. The 'ln' at the end stands for line. This means after printing what you place in the parentheses the function will make a new line to print the next expression. The 'print' function will simply print whatever you put in the parenthesis without introducing its own formatting.

Chapter 2:
Input and Output

In this chapter we're going to look more closely at input and output, which are perhaps the two most critical activities in any program. In the previous chapter we looked closely at the output we produced with the println command. With println we were able to output three types of data to the command line screen: strings, integers, and floating point numbers. The programs we wrote, however, had no capacity to take input and process data.

In this chapter we're going to look closely at two types of input. First input statements will allow us to programmatically request input from the user. We'll then use command line parameters to provide inputs to our program.

As we look at output, we'll also look at directing our output to a file instead of back to the command line.

So now it's time to put on your favorite programming music (I suggest The Cure), open **nano**, **vi** or your favorite text editor and start coding...

Input Statements

We're going to start with a program that calculates the area of a rectangle based on a *sideA* input and a *sideB* input. Key the following Java code into your text editor:

```java
import java.util.Scanner;

public class Square{
  public static void main (String[] args) {

    System.out.println("RECTANGLE AREA CALCULATOR");

    Scanner input = new Scanner(System.in);

    System.out.println("What's the length of side A? ");
    float sideA = input.nextFloat();

    System.out.println("What's the length of side B? ");
    float sideB = input.nextFloat();

    float area = sideA*sideB;

    System.out.println("The area of your rectangle is: " + area);
```

Once you are sure you have keyed in the program correctly and saved it, go ahead and run the program on the command line. I saved mine as **Square.java**. Your output should look similar to figure 2.1:

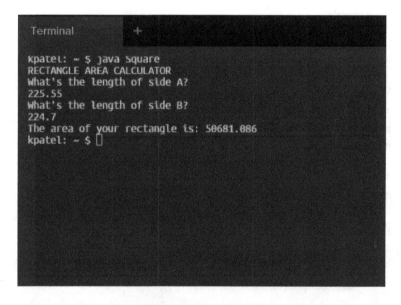

```
Terminal                    +

kpatel: ~ $ java Square
RECTANGLE AREA CALCULATOR
What's the length of side A?
225.55
What's the length of side B?
224.7
The area of your rectangle is: 50681.086
kpatel: ~ $ 
```

Figure 2.1: Execution of the Square.java program which takes input from the user via the Java **.nextFloat()** function.

On the first line of this program, we encounter the **import** statement. Imports are used in many languages to add an additional library of commands to the language that are not in the language core. In this case, we're adding the **Scanner** object from the **util** library which contains a number of utilities and useful objects.

If you want to import the entire library, all you have to do is replace Scanner with an asterisk (*).

For example:

import java.util.*;

While this is useful, understand that in much larger programs importing an entire library just to get one object like we're doing here makes your program less efficient. It's like grabbing your whole tool box when you just need a hammer.

Now, based on context and the program execution, you've probably already guessed what the **nextInt()** function does. Let's break it down:

```
public static void main (String[] args) {

    Scanner grabAge = new Scanner(System.in);

    System.out.println("How old are you?");

    int age = grabAge.nextInt();

}
```

The first line of this class creates a Scanner object. Scanners are the object we use to obtain input from the command line.

In the example above, whatever the user types at the prompt "*How old are you?*" is going to be assigned to the variable **age** via the Scanner's nextInt method. We're going to take a closer look at variables in the next chapter—for right now, just consider variables a temporary storage place for values. These values can be strings, floats, or integers. You must declare variables before using them. Generally the syntax is the datatype followed by a name to reference the variable.

You may be wondering what a datatype is. Datatype determines what a variable can contain, and what operations can be performed on it. Some examples of datatypes include integers, strings, and floating point numbers.

Here's an example of the declaration of an integer variable:

int name;

Note: Int indicates that the datatype for this variable is an integer.

Remember to import the Scanner object or the util library before declaring a Scanner object. Otherwise, your program will encounter an error.

Let's try a new example. Create a new file in your text editor called StringInput.java. You can do this in vi, for example, by typing the following command on the command line: **vi StringInput.java**.

Key in the following code:

```
import java.util.Scanner;

public class StringInput{
```

```
public static void main (String[] args) {

    Scanner input = new Scanner(System.in);
    System.out.println("What's your name? ");

    String name = input.nextFloat();

    System.out.println("Hello " + name);
  }
}
```

Exit your text editor and compile the program from your command line with the command **javac StringInput.java**.

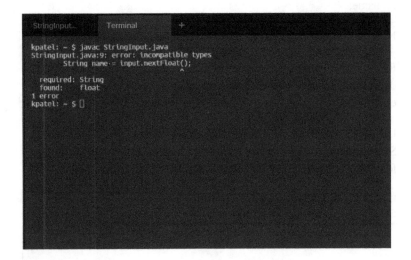

Figure 2.2: Uh-oh. This can't be good. We've made an error. How do we fix it?

So what happened? Instead of compiling and allowing the code to run, the program exited with an error. Luckily the error is easy to fix. The nextFloat() function is designed to accept the float datatype and only that datatype. When you enter anything that isn't a floating point number, it causes the error you see in figure 2.2. We have a different function that is intended for string use, called **nextLine()**.

Edit your code as follows:

```
import java.util.Scanner;
public class StringInput{

    public static void main (String[] args) {

        Scanner input = new Scanner(System.in);
        System.out.println("What's your name?
");

        String name = input.nextLine();

        System.out.println("Hello " + name);
    }
}
```

Note: The scanner has a function to obtain every kind of data type.

Here are some examples:

nextLine() : Strings

nextInt(): Integers

nextFloat(): Floating point numbers

nextDouble(): Doubles

You can probably recognize the pattern. The documentation of the methods for the Scanner object is available here:

http://docs.oracle.com/Javase/7/docs/api/Java/util/Scanner.html

Learning how to read the Java documentation is an important skill itself.

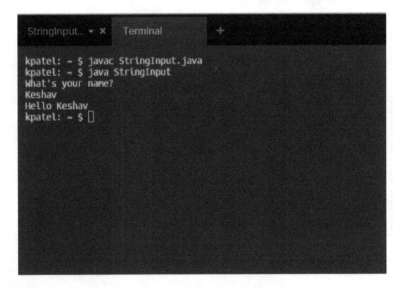

Figure 2.3: So much better with nextLine()!

When you're working with strings, you should use the **nextLine()** function which does not scan for a datatype other than Strings. It'll always return whatever the user enter into the prompt as a string, including numbers or symbols.

Errors

The preceding example was probably one of the first examples of an error that you've encountered. This type of error is known as a Runtime error. It's one of three types of errors that can occur when writing Java code.

These three types are:

Syntax errors:

Syntax errors are issues with the formatting of your code. Examples include forgetting semicolons, not closing your brackets or misspelling method names. Text editors generally do a great job of pointing these out, so fixing them is rather simple.

Runtime errors:

Runtime errors are a bit trickier to catch. Syntactically, all runtime errors are correct, so your text editor won't point them out to you. The issue occurs when something unexpected happens and results in the program failing to execute *at runtime*. The result is your program fails to compile or execute properly. Examples include trying to divide by zero or trying to call up a file that doesn't exist. Java won't encounter the error until it attempts to execute the code.

Logic errors:

These are errors in the actual logic behind the program. They are the most challenging errors to fix, because the code isn't technically wrong, it's just not giving the correct result. Some logical errors go undetected even after the program is released. Examples include things like dividing where you should be multiplying, printing the wrong output, or opening the wrong file. If you have a logic error, you're having a PICNIC. (Problem In Chair, Not In Computer.)

Parameterized Input

Your current workflow forces you to compile and then run your code before passing input. Including parameters with your Java command passes input and executes your code in tandem. The resulting command looks like this:

$ java ClassName arg1 arg2 arg3

In the example above, we still use the Java command and the class name of the program we'd like to run. We follow the class name with arguments which get sent as input to the program. This could be advantageous in situations where we want our program to run unattended- like when we're crunching numbers. For example, if we wanted a program to receive the users name and age as input, the parameters might look something like this:

$ java moreInput Keshav 17

The values "Keshav" and "17", which are separated by a single space, are passed to the program. Let's see how. Key in the following example and save it as **MoreInput.java**:

```
public class MoreInput{

   public static void main (String[] args) {

      System.out.println("Your name is: " + args[0]);
      System.out.println("Your age is: " + args[1]);

      System.out.println("All the arguments: ");

      System.out.println(args[0] + ", " + args[1]);
   }
}
```

Next, let's run the program and supply command line arguments as input:

$ java MoreInput Keshav 17

You should get a result similar to the one pictured in figure 2.4:

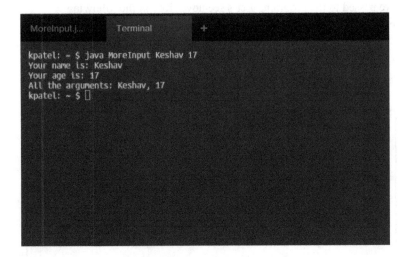

```
kpatel: ~ $ java MoreInput Keshav 17
Your name is: Keshav
Your age is: 17
All the arguments: Keshav, 17
kpatel: ~ $ []
```

Figure 2.4: Command line parameters being processed as input on the Koding command line.

NOTE: The terms parameter and argument can be used interchangeably.

The arguments come into Java numbered sequentially, so in our case, the user's name is argument number zero and the age is argument number one. In code, we call these **args[0]** and **args[1],** respectively. If you study the screenshot carefully, you may notice something interesting-- **args[1]** is *not* the first parameter.

This is because Java starts counting at 0, rather than 1. This means that the first argument we entered, which in this case was a name, is actually in slot 0. As a result Java is often referred to as a zero-indexed language.

Output to a Filestream

So far the code's output has only been directed to the command line. This doesn't always have to be the case. Output can be directed to a file for more permanent storage. Being able to store data (more or less) permanently is an important skill for programmers to learn. Let's write a program in which we ask the user to enter several pieces of data and we then store those in a file.

Key in the following code:

```java
import java.io.*;
import java.util.Scanner;
public class Storage{

    public static void main (String[] args) {

        Scanner grab  = new Scanner(System.in);


        System.out.println("What's your name?");
        String name = grab.nextLine();
```

```
            System.out.println("What's your email?");
            String mail = grab.nextLine();

            System.out.println("What's your favorite
band?");
            String band = grab.nextLine();

            String fname = name.replaceAll("
","")+".txt";

            try{
                PrintWriter saver = new
PrintWriter(fname);

                saver.println("Name:" + name);
                saver.println("Email:" + mail);
                saver.println("Band:" + band);
                saver.close();
            }
            catch(FileNotFoundException e){
                System.out.println("Oh no, it didn't
work!");
            }
            System.out.println(name + "|" + mail + "|"
+ band + " has been stored to "+ name + ".txt.");
        }
    }
```

This is definitely the most complex program we've written yet. Go ahead and run it on the command line and make sure you don't get any errors. If you're having issues remember to check the imports. If everything runs correctly, your command line should look something like this:

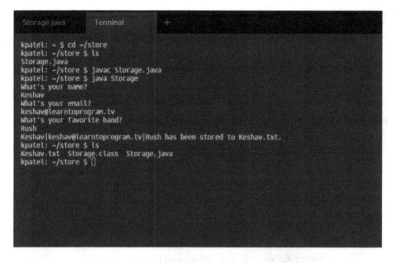

```
kpatel: ~ $ cd ~/store
kpatel: ~/store $ ls
Storage.java
kpatel: ~/store $ javac Storage.java
kpatel: ~/store $ java Storage
What's your name?
Keshav
What's your email?
keshav@learntoprogram.tv
What's your favorite band?
Rush
Keshav|keshav@learntoprogram.tv|Rush has been stored to Keshav.txt.
kpatel: ~/store $ ls
Keshav.txt  Storage.class  Storage.java
kpatel: ~/store $ []
```

Figure 2.5: The program stored the data in a file called Keshav.txt which is now available in the directory listing by using the *ls* command on the command line.

Note: I wrote and saved the file in a separate folder, and needed to navigate to where the file was beforehand using the cd (change directory) command.

While the code for this program is somewhat longer than what you are used to at this point, it is still fairly straightforward. When the program runs it prompts the user for their name, email, and name of their favorite band. We then create a new variable called saver. Saver takes the information the user typed and formats it to increase readability. It then prints the information to a file.

The objects we use to print to a file are located in the Java.io library and we're going to need a couple of objects, so import the whole thing.

The fname variable, which stores the filename for the file we're creating, is populated by the variable that holds the user's first name. When we create the new PrintWriter object, we pass in the filename. This is required so the PrintWriter knows what to name the file it creates.

The next part of the program is where the action happens:

```java
public static void main (String[] args) {

  try{
       PrintWriter saver = new PrintWriter(fname);

       saver.println("Name:" + name);
       saver.println("Email:" + mail);
       saver.println("Band:" + band);
       saver.close();
    }
  catch(FileNotFoundException e){
       System.out.println("Oh no, it didn't work!");
    }
  System.out.println(name + "|" + mail + "|" + band + " has been stored
to "+ name +        ".txt.");
  }
}
```

The first thing we do in the program is create a **PrintWriter**. This is an object that allows us to create and then print to raw text (.txt) files. We named it saver and pass in the string fname as a parameter. When the writer created our file, this string became the file's name. Next we use our PrintWriter object and began printing strings to the text file. Finally we closed the object and printed to the console that we have created a file with the information that the user provided us with.

Note that this entire process is done within a try-catch statement. A try-catch statement is used to handle exceptions, which are events that interfere with the execution of your program. In the try block we put code that could possibly cause (AKA throw) an exception. In the catch block, we put code that executes if an exception is thrown. The parentheses contain the type of exception and the name we give it. In this case we just print "Oh no, it didn't work!" in the event that we get an exception.

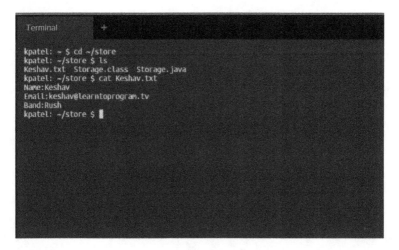

Figure 2.6 We opened "Keshav.txt" in the text editor and you can see the data that has been written to the disk.

Congratulations! You've written a program that stores data permanently. You are well on your way to being a programmer!

Chapter 3:
Variables

In the previous chapter, we looked at input and output, which allow us to get data into and out of our Java program. In this chapter we'll take a closer look at one of the most important aspects of programming—variables. You may not equate variables with computer programming, but you've likely been using variables since high school if you took courses in Algebra, Chemistry, and Physics. In classic "solve for x" problems, x is a variable.

Let's first take a look at how the Java programming environment handles variables.

Declaring and Initializing Variables

Java is what is known as a strongly-typed language. This means that variables need to be declared before they can be used. In Java, variables are differentiated by the type of data they hold. The type of data is referred to the variable's datatype.

There are two types of variables in Java: primitive type and class (also called reference) type.

Primitive Variables

In Java, there are eight primitive data types. They are the byte, short, int, long, float, double, boolean and chars.

The declaration and initialization statements are generally very short, and reserve a specific amount of memory depending on what type the variable is. Here's an example of a declaration and initialization for an integer, done in one line:

int name = 93;

Class Variables

Class type variables, also called reference type variables, are generally more complex than primitive types. In most cases primitive types are the building blocks of class type variables. When you declare and initialize a class type variable, the name doesn't represent the object itself, rather it points to the memory location that has all of the parts and information that make up the object.

There are hundreds of different class type variables out there, and they all do different things. One you've already encountered is a Scanner.

Here's the declaration and initialization, one more time:

Scanner name = new Scanner(<parameters>);

Strings

Strings in Java are actually class or reference type variables. They can, however, be declared like primitives. This was a sort of short cut put in by the Java developers to make dealing with strings a bit easier, as they're one of the most common datatypes and are used just as much as the primitives. (Think about how much you've used them already!)

If you like, you can declare strings like you would class type variables, but there's really no advantage in doing so.

It would look like this:

```
String blogName = new String("Edukwest!");
```

NOTE: Due to strings being class type, they cannot be compared like primitive types using the general comparison operators like <,> or ==.

Here, we've created a variable called **blogName** and initialized it with the string value "Edukwest!" The equals sign in this context is the assignment operator. The string value "Edukwest!" is being assigned to the variable **blogName**.

Once a variable has been declared, generally you can do quite a lot with it. Here's an example of using variables to change what is printed in a sentence.

Key in the following code. (Feel free to substitute your own values for the variables.) Notice that comments are indicated by two slashes (//).
Multi-line comments can be made with a slash and an asterisk and closed with an asterisk and a slash. (/*comment!*/)

```java
public class Variables{

    public static void main (String[] args) {

        float gpa = 3.95f;
        int age = 17;
        String name = "Keshav";

        //Note that the first word of the variable
declaration is the type.

        System.out.println(name + " is " + age + " and
wished he had a " + gpa + " gpa.");

    }

}
```

Save your file as Variables.java and run it with the Java command. Your output should appear similar to figure 3.1

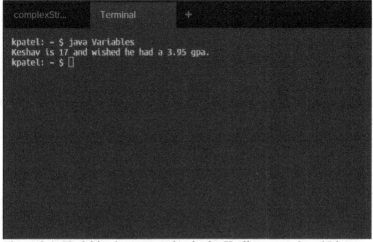

```
kpatel: ~ $ java Variables
Keshav is 17 and wished he had a 3.95 gpa.
kpatel: ~ $ []
```

Figure 3.1: Variables.java executing in the Koding.com virtual Linux environment.

The first word in the declaration is the type of variable being created. To review, the types of variables in this program are:

String: String variables are comprised of a series of characters in a particular order that have no mathematical value.

Integer: Integer variables contain whole number values with no decimal point.

Floating Point Values: Floating point variables contain more precise numbers that have a whole number and fractional amount represented by a decimal point value.

Variables are dynamic, in that the value can be changed or reassigned through the life of the program. Imagine, for example, that in a video game you have a variable that tracks the player's score. As the player's score changes, that value would go up until the game is over. Once the game ends, the value inside the player's score variable might be reassigned the value zero.

Consider the following code:

```
import java.util.*;
public class Var2{

    public static void main (String[] args) {
        Scanner names = new Scanner(System.in);

        String firstName, lastName, middleName,
fullName;

        System.out.println("What's your first
name?");
        firstName = names.nextLine();

        System.out.println("What's your last
name?");
        lastName = names.nextLine();
```

```
        fullName = firstName +" "+ lastName;

        System.out.println(fullName);

        System.out.println("What's your middle
name?");

        middleName = names.nextLine();

        fullName = firstName + " " + middleName + "
" + lastName;

        System.out.println(fullName);

    }

  }
```

Entering the code and running the program yields the following result:

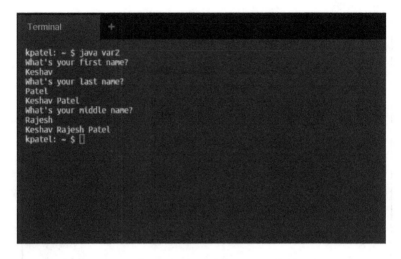

```
Terminal                    +

kpatel: ~ $ java var2
What's your first name?
Keshav
What's your last name?
Patel
Keshav Patel
What's your middle name?
Rajesh
Keshav Rajesh Patel
kpatel: ~ $ 
```

Figure 3.2: During the lifetime of the fullName variable, the value is reassigned

Note that when we first declare the **fullName** variable, it is assigned the values of **first** and **last** concatenated by the + sign. That value is then printed to the console. As the program continues to execute, the value of **fullName** is reassigned to include the variable **middle** as well. When a variable is assigned a new value, its original value is cleared and replaced with the new value.

In this program, we also declared four Strings in one line. Due to all the variables being of the String type, we were able to separate the four string's names with commas, and assign them values later on. Being a statically typed language, Java requires us to declare our variables before use. Being a statically-typed language doesn't necessarily mean we have to assign initial values (or initialize) the variables upon declaration.

You can do this with all types of variables.

Arithmetic with Variables

Variables are frequently used as part of arithmetic expressions in Java. Arithmetic in Java is no different than the arithmetic you learned in grade school. The following symbols are used:

+   Addition

- Subtraction

*   Multiplication

/ Division

%   Modulus

If you are new to programming, modulus may be unfamiliar to you, but the concept is easy—modulus is the remainder after division. For example:

10 % 3 = 1

11 % 3 = 2

$12 \% 3 = 0$

I frequently use modulus when programming in order to determine if a number is even or odd. Any even number used with modulus two will result in zero.

Talk the Talk: *Most programmers will say 'mod' for short when they are talking about modulus.*

Math with variables looks pretty much as you'd expect. There are a few oddities that we'll cover later though.

Key in the following example program. You're free to forgo copying the comments:

```java
    public class MathDemo{
        public static void main (String[] args) {

            int alpha = 3;
            int bravo = 13;

            System.out.println(alpha + bravo);
            System.out.println(alpha - bravo);
            System.out.println(bravo * alpha);
            System.out.println(bravo / alpha); //Note:
13/3 is not really a whole number.
            System.out.println(bravo % alpha);
```

```
        System.out.println((double)bravo/(double)alp
ha);
        /* Because we've casted the numbers as
doubles, the real value is displayed. */


    }


  }
```

In this program, two variables are declared as alpha and bravo. Then the operands are put in five expressions using addition, subtraction, multiplication, division and modulus.

Both of these numbers, however, are integers. Integers can only be whole numbers between $(2^{31})-1$ or -2^{31}. So expressions of the integer datatype have any numbers after the decimal point truncated.

This means that if an expression results in 3.9, but is printed as an int, it'll simply print 3.

We can avoid this issue by doing what's known as type casting. This changes the variable's type just before doing the math and printing, meaning we'll get the real answer rather than an approximation.

Java requires you to identify the types of your variables. When using variables of different types together, you may have to explicitly state what type of variable you want the answer to be.

As a rule of thumb: small variables types automatically transfer up, but large variables must manually be casted down.

This is the hierarchy:

  byte < short < int < long < float < double

Using an int with a float requires no typecasting. Getting an answer as an int with a float and int DOES require you to explicitly cast your variable.

A final print statement uses the modulus statement in an expression. When you run the program with the Java command, the result should appear similar to this:

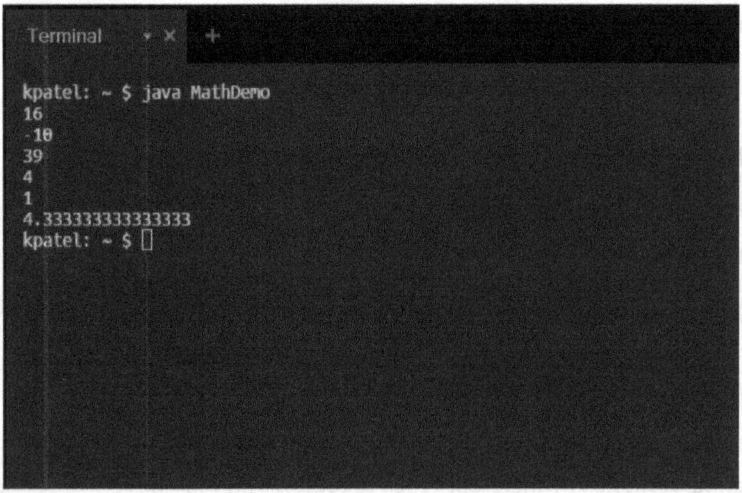

```
kpatel: ~ $ java MathDemo
16
-10
39
4
1
4.333333333333333
kpatel: ~ $ ▯
```

Figure 3.3: Java program evaluating several mathematical expressions and outputting the result to the console.

When working with arithmetic in programming, it's important to keep in mind the order of operations. Java will always follow the order of operations when doing math. As a result it's a good idea to make sure that any expressions you formulate take into account the order of operations to prevent logic errors.

Figure 3.4: Different expressions are evaluated in a Java program demonstrating the order of operations.

Was the result always what you expected? The order of operations determines what part of a mathematical expression is evaluated first. Expressions are evaluated from left to right generally, but the specific order of operations is:

1) Parenthesis
2) Exponents
3) Multiplication
4) Division
5) Addition
6) Subtraction

NOTE: Despite multiplication coming before division and addition coming before subtraction, Java treats them as though they are on the same level and evaluates them left to right.

A common error made by new programmers is to incorrectly interpret the order of operations within a math-related problem. When this happens, a program will still run, but often give an incorrect result.

There are many more advanced mathematics tools available in Java within the Math class. Utilizing this class will allow you to round numbers, use exponents, square roots, and much more. The documentation is available here:
http://docs.oracle.com/Javase/7/docs/api/Java/lang/Math.html

Working with Strings

Manipulating strings is a common task for programmers. Imagine, for example, you're given a list of data where first and last names are combined into a single field. Using string manipulation techniques, you'd have to separate them into separate fields by extracting data from the string.

Java's String Methods will allow you to manipulate strings in every way imaginable. You can see the documentation on the String Methods here: http://docs.oracle.com/Javase/7/docs/api/Java/lang/String.html

Let's work with a few String Methods. Copy the following program. This program demonstrates just a few of the string functions. You don't have to type the embedded comments if you don't want to. They are just for your reference.

```java
public class Strings{

    public static void main (String[] args) {

        String phrase = "The quick brown fox jumped over the lazy dogs.";


        //Prints the number of characters in the String
        System.out.println(phrase.length());

        //Finds the index of the word fox.
        System.out.println(phrase.indexOf("fox"));

        //Replace jumped with a new word.
        System.out.println(phrase.replace("jumped" , "hopped"));
```

```
//Changes case
System.out.println(phrase.toUpperCase());
System.out.println(phrase.toLowerCase());

        }
}
```

Once you run the program, you should see a result similar figure 3.5:

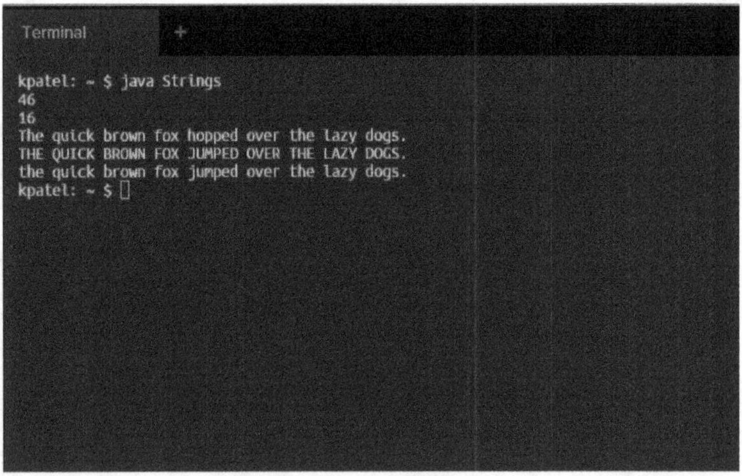

Figure 3.5: String manipulation result in Java

As you can see, Java's string manipulation features are powerful.

Chapter 4:
Conditionals and Loops

In the last chapter we took a close look at variables. In this chapter, we're going to use variables again. First, we'll use variables to make decisions and execute branching within our program. Then we'll use variables to create loops that iterate through a portion of code a number of times. Conditionals and loops, the two concepts that we haven't covered up to now, are found in just about every programming language. So far, the programs we've written are all serial—they go through the same steps in the same order each time. With the addition of conditionals and loops to our programming repertoire, your programs will be able to vary their path based on conditions you set. Sounds like fun, right?

Simple Conditionals

Let's start by writing some code. Fire up your development environment and enter the following code (Make sure the file and class names match):

```java
import java.util.*;

public class Drink{

    public static void main (String[] args) {

        Scanner ageGetter = new Scanner(System.in);

        System.out.println("How old are you?");

        int age = ageGetter.nextInt();

        if(age >= 21){
            System.out.println("You can legally drink!");
        }

    }

}
```

Once you've entered the program in your text editor, run it three separate times. The first time, enter an age older than 21. The next time you run it, enter an age younger than 21. When you run it one final time, enter 21 exactly. To make sure the program runs correctly we want to test all the possible scenarios for execution.

Your output should appear similar to figure 4.1:

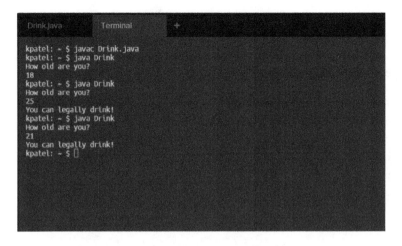

Figure 4.1: Program being tested for three different types of user responses

This program is pretty straightforward. What's new is the *if* statement. In this case we're determining if the value the user entered is *greater than or equal to* 21. The portion of the if statement written like this: age>=21 is known as the *condition*. Every conditional statement has a condition that is evaluated to be *true* or *false*. If it's true, the code indented underneath and in brackets the conditional statement is executed. If it's false generally it's skipped.

Note in the example shown in figure 4.1, the program responds "You are legally able to drink" only if the user enters a value 21 or greater.

Java uses brackets to contain blocks of code, so after you open the bracket make sure you close it back up or else your program won't compile properly. Make sure that you only keep the code you want to execute within the brackets of the conditional.

If the code block that runs if the condition is true extends more than one line, please note that each line should be within the brackets of the conditional. It's also good practice to have the same level of indentation below the conditional statement. It won't affect how the code runs, but it makes the code look much cleaner. Other programmers reading your code will thank you.

What Else?

The program we wrote responds only if the conditional is evaluated as true. If the conditional is evaluated as false, the user receives no response. This is likely confusing for the user. We're going to add to the program so that it reacts one way if the condition is evaluated as true and another way if the condition is evaluated as false. Add the indicated code to your class.

```
import java.util.*;

public class Drink{

    public static void main (String[] args) {
```

```
Scanner ageGetter = new Scanner(System.in);

System.out.println("How old are you?");

int age = ageGetter.nextInt();

if(age >= 21){
    System.out.println("You can legally drink!");
}
else{
    System.out.println("You're not of drinking age.");
}


}


}
```

After modifying your program code, run through the three possible scenarios as you did before. Test a case where the user is under 21, another where the user is older than 21, and a final scenario where the user is exactly 21. Your output should appear similar to figure 4.2:

Don't forget to save and recompile!

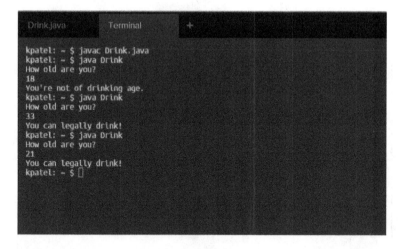

Figure 4.2 Result with the else statement added

As you can tell, the addition of the *else* statement gave a result if a value under 21 was entered. When the user enters a value under 21, the condition is evaluated as false and the else statement block is triggered. Once again, only the code in the brackets is considered part of the statement block.

Let's add a little bit more code to our program:

```java
import java.util.*;

public class Drink{

    public static void main (String[] args) {

        Scanner ageGetter = new Scanner(System.in);

        System.out.println("How old are you?");

        int age = ageGetter.nextInt();

        if(age >= 21){
            System.out.println("You can legally drink!");
        }
        else{
            System.out.println("You're not of drinking age.");
        }
        if(age == 21){
            System.out.println("Congratulations, Here's a free drink.");
        }


    }


}
```

Now, if the user says they are exactly 21, the program will print the congratulatory message. Note that the comparison operator == was used to denote equality. If the value in age is exactly 21, the conditional is evaluated as true.

Here are all the comparison operators that you can use with if statements:

==   Equal

>   Greater Than

>=   Greater Than or Equal

<   Less Than

<=   Less Than or Equal

!=   Not Equal

Note: these operators can only be used for primitive types like ints or floats! For reference types there is generally a method that can be used to compare elements instead. Usually it's the **.equals()** method.

While you can already see the power of conditionals, let's add a layer of complexity: what if you wanted to test two values at once?

Compound Conditionals

Let's pretend that we're writing software for a college to determine whether or not a specific student made the honor roll. In our college, in order to be eligible for honors you must both have a GPA greater than 3.5 and attempt more than 12 credit hours.

Create a new program in your text editor called Honors.java and enter the code below in the file:

```java
import java.util.*;

public class Honors{

    public static void main (String[] args) {

        Scanner gpaGet = new Scanner(System.in);

        Scanner hoursGet = new Scanner(System.in);


        System.out.println("What was your GPA this semester?");
        double gpa = gpaGet.nextDouble();

        System.out.println("How many credit hours did you attempt this semester?");
        int hours = hoursGet.nextInt();

        if(gpa>3.5 && hours > 12){
            System.out.println("Congratulations! You made honor roll!");
        }
        else{
```

```
                    System.out.println("Sorry, you didn't
make honor roll. Better luck next time.");
            }
        }

    }
```

Test your program and see what kind of result you get. Your result should be similar to what appears in figure 4.3:

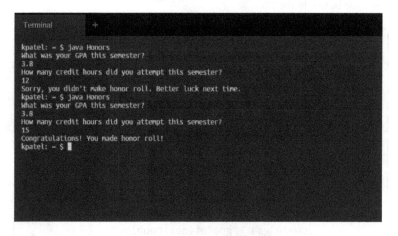

Figure 4.3: Two conditions are tested simultaneously.

You'll notice that in the **if** statement we joined two conditions by two amperstamps (&&), which, in this case, is acting as an operator. In this if statement both conditions joined by && must be evaluated as true in order for the whole statement to be evaluated as true. You can use two vertical bars (||) as an operator in other circumstances where one condition or the other must be true. You can join any amount of conditions in a single if statement with **&&** and || operators.

Talk the Talk: Generally when reading code, a programmer will read '&&' as "and" and will read '||' as "or". So the line if (a>b && c<d || d<c) will be read as "if a is greater than b and c is less than d, or if d is less than c (the condition is) true".

Complex Conditionals with else-if

So far the conditionals we've created can make decisions in an either/or scenario—either you are eligible to drink, or you're not. However, life is more complex than this, which is why if statements can be paired with else-if statements. This combination will let you choose from several options as in the program below.

Please key in this program and run it with the Java command to see the result:

```java
import java.util.*;

public class ComplexConditionals{

    public static void main (String[] args) {

        Scanner ageGet = new Scanner(System.in);

        System.out.println("How old are you?");
```

```java
        int age = ageGet.nextInt();

        if(age < 18){
            System.out.println("You're a kid!");
            System.out.println("Go to school.");
        }
        else if(age < 29){
            System.out.println("Time to establish
yourself.");
            System.out.println("Good Luck!");
        }
        else if(age < 39){
            System.out.println("These are the years
to focus on your career.");
            System.out.println("Get a job.");

        }
        else if(age < 49){
            System.out.println("Time to start
thinking about retirement.");
            System.out.println("I hope you're
putting money away.");
        }
        else if(age < 59){
            System.out.println("Maintain your
health through exercise.");
            System.out.println("Get a trainer.");
        }
        else{
            System.out.println("You are old");
        }

    }
}
```

With apologies to those 59 and older, this program provides feedback based on the age the user enters. First the user enters their age and this value is assigned to the variable *age*. The value entered by the user is then tested in the first part of the if statement. If the age is less than 18, the program responds with "You're a kid! Go to school."

If the first condition turns out to be false, the *else if* condition is evaluated. If the age is less than 29 the appropriate advice is dispensed. If not, the next statement is evaluated. If none of the conditions associated with the *else if* statements are found to be true, then the unfortunate *else* statement at the end of the program runs.

Keep in mind that *else if* statements are only run if all of the previous conditions are found to be false. Note also the indentation used throughout the *else/else if/else* is consistent. This is for housekeeping purposes. Readability is a important part of programming.

While Loops

Loops allow you to run a block of code a number of times. Each time that block of code is executed is known as an *iteration*. Loops are critical to many different types of programs. Imagine a card game where turns are taken and cards are dealt—all with loops. If you think about it, you can probably identify loops in many different types of software that you use every day. The process of waiting for the user to input something, processing that input and then waiting for the user again is often coded in a loop structure.

Let's code a simple loop:

```java
public class Loop{

    public static void main (String[] args) {

        int tracker = 0;

        while(tracker<100){

            System.out.println(tracker);

            tracker += 5;
        }

    }

}
```

Run the program with the Java command and the result should appear
something like what you see in figure 4.4:

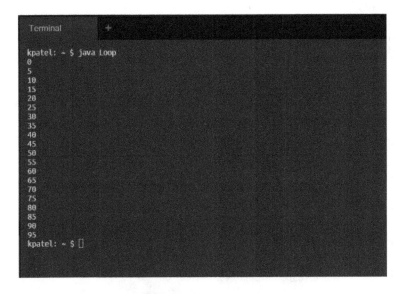

```
kpatel: ~ $ java Loop
0
5
10
15
20
25
30
35
40
45
50
55
60
65
70
75
80
85
90
95
kpatel: ~ $ ▯
```

Figure 4.4: The result of a while loop

In the first line of this program we declare and initialize a variable *tracker* with the value 0. Next comes our *while* statement which states that while the value of *tracker* is less than 100, the code block inside the brackets of the *while* statement will execute. In this case, the code block prints the value of *tracker* to the console and then increases the value *tracker* by 5.

Note that the x+=5 notation is shorthand for x=x+5. += is known as a combined assignment operator.

Talk the Talk: Programmers generally call "+=" "plus equals". So when describing this code one would say "x plus equals five"

Here's another loop example program for you to try. I saved mine as Loop2.java.

```java
import java.util.*;

public class Loop2{

    public static void main (String[] args) {

        Scanner bandName = new Scanner(System.in);
        String band = "";

        while(!band.equals("XXX")){

            System.out.println("Name of a band you like or XXX to stop.");
            band = bandName.nextLine();

            if(!band.equals("XXX")){
                System.out.println( band + " ROCKS!");
            }
        }

    }

}
```

Note: Due to strings being a reference type, you have to use the .equals() method to check for equality. This method returns true if the strings are equal and false if not.

Run the program with the Java command and you should see a result similar to figure 4.5:

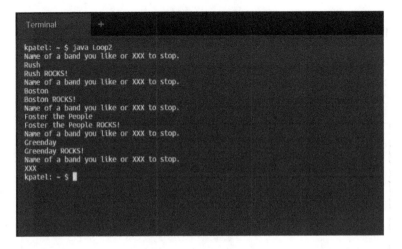

Figure 4.5 The user inputs text inside a loop.

When this program initially runs, the variable *band* is set to an empty string. The value of *band* is compared to the string "XXX" each time through the loop. If the loop is anything other than "XXX" the loop iterates again. If the value is not XXX, the name of the band is echoed back to the console.

Notice that all of the opening brackets have a companion. If you get lost in code that has a number of closing brackets in a row, here's a trick:

There always must be the same number of opening and closing brackets in a class – If you have more opening brackets try pairing each one off until you where find you're missing closing brackets.

Don't Try This at Home

A common error in programming is an endless loop. These endless loops can consume more and more computing resources and eventually make the program, or your computer crash. Consider the following code:

```
public class LetsBreakTheComputer{

  public static void main (String[] args) {

    double x = 1;

    while(0<x){

      System.out.println(x);

      X*=300000;
    }

  }

}
```

You'll note that the continuation condition will **always** be true in this example—the value of x will always be greater than zero. The value of x very rapidly gets out of hand and, in fact, becomes too big to store in memory. I ran this in the Koding.com environment. It took me about 10 minutes to stop the execution of the program as koding's environment was lagging due to the program.

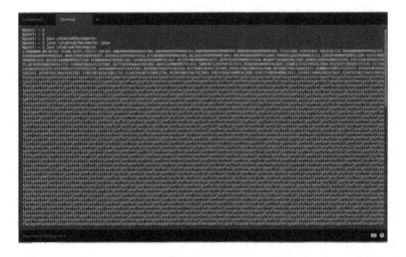

Figure 4.6: At this point the environment was frozen due to an endless loop. Every so often it would print "Infinity" a couple hundred times and then freeze right back up.

You can try this example on your own. I'm not responsible for any damage done. (Damage won't be permanent…have fun!)

For loops

So we've determined that forgetting to put a proper iterator in your while loop can be bad for your program. How can we avoid having an endless while loop? The answer is a for loop. For loops do the same thing as while loops, however they will only execute a set number of times because you are forced to place an iterator and variable as part of the loop's syntax in addition to a conditional. As a result it's extremely difficult to create a for loop that executes endlessly.

Here's an example of a very simple for loop. It does the same thing as our first loop: Prints 0 to 100, while counting by fives.

This loop is in a file called Loop3:

```
public class Loop3{

    public static void main (String[] args) {

        for(int x = 0; x<100; x+=5){
            System.out.println(x);
        }

    }

}
```

The syntax of the loop is simple. First we have a local variable x that is initialized and declared. Local variables cannot be accessed or changed outside of the loop. Then, we have a conditional. The conditional fulfills the same purpose as in the while loop. When it is no longer true the loop will stop iterating. Finally we have what's known as an iterator. This is a reassignment of the variable you initially declared for this loop. The iterator is the reason that it's generally hard to accidently make an endless loop. Note that these three statements are separated by semicolons as though they were the end of lines. Here's the result of executing this code:

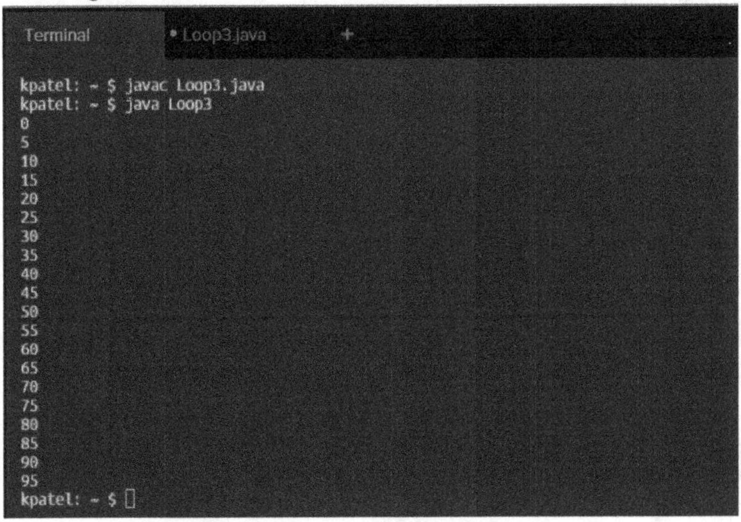
Terminal
• Loop3.java
kpatel: ~ $ javac Loop3.java
kpatel: ~ $ java Loop3
0
5
10
15
20
25
30
35
40
45
50
55
60
65
70
75
80
85
90
95
kpatel: ~ $

Figure 4.7: The result of the for loop is the same as the result of our original while loop.

Chapter 5:
Dealing with Data

In the last chapter we examined control structures, conditionals, and loops, which are critical in most programming languages. They allow your programs to make decisions based on the criteria that you set as the developer. In this chapter, we're going to switch gears and examine data and how it's stored. We'll take a close look at four data structures: Arrays, ArrayLists, Immutables, and HashTables. You may not have given much thought to data before. The easiest way to conceptualize data is as organized information.

Different types of information lend itself to being organized in different ways. For example, if your data is a grocery list, then an Array would be the optimal way to organize your data. However, if you wanted to store student grades on different assignments over a period of time, an Array wouldn't work well at all. There are many different data structures used by programmers and each is optimized for a different type of data.

Let's start with a simple grocery list.

Arrays

We've all made a grocery list before, but you likely haven't stored it in Java code. Let's do that now using the following line of code: (Remember to put this in your main method!)

```
String[] groceries = {
            "oranges","apples","milk","bread","butter","pepp
er","salt","sugar","pears"
        };
```

Unlike variables which store a single unit of data, we've stored multiple elements in our array. I'm sure you can imagine a number of situations where this could be convenient. In this case, all of the *members* or elements of our array are strings. This is because we declared our array as a String array. "String" is the data type of the array's members.

Here is another array to add to your code. This time it's comprised of double values:

```
double[] gpas = {
            3.25, 2.26, 1.99, 3.55, 4.0, 3.21, 2.56, 3.06 ,
2.72
        };
```

Now, here's where arrays become a bit more interesting. Arrays have a number of built-in methods that you can use to manipulate them; There are included functions that do things like count the members of the list or sort them. You could write your own code to do all this, but it would be a lot of work.

Before we start with the really fancy stuff, let's take a look at how we extract data from the Array. Go ahead and copy the code below. You're free to skip over the comments if you like. Remember to keep the file name and the class name consistent!

```java
public class Arrays{

    public static void main (String[] args) {

        String[] groceries = {
            "oranges","apples","milk","bread","butter","pepper","salt","sugar","pears"
        };

        double[] gpas = {
            3.25, 2.26, 1.99, 3.55, 4.0, 3.21, 2.56, 3.06 , 2.72
        };

        System.out.println(groceries[0]); //returns 'oranges'

        System.out.println(groceries[1]); // returns 'apples'

        System.out.println(gpas[3]); // returns '3.55'

    }

}
```

Once you're sure that the code is typed correctly in your text editor, execute the code with the **Java** command. Don't forget to compile! Your output should look like this:

Figure 5.1: Java Arrays program output using the Koding.com environment

Pay special attention to the print statements. You'll note that each print statement references one of our arrays and a specific index within that list surrounded by brackets. Lists in Java, like most languages, are indexed, meaning that each member of the list is assigned a number used to reference it. The first member of a list is always index zero.

Our grocery list would have the following indexes:

Index	Member
0	oranges

1	apples
2	milk
3	bread
4	butter
5	pepper
6	salt
7	sugar
8	pears

When combined with print method, the general form of retrieving data from an array is:

ArrayName[#];

Where "#" is the index you are pointing to.

One thing to keep in mind is that your array is only as long as you initially make it. If you try to access a non-existent array index, your program is going to exit with an error. Let's add one line to our current program:

```
System.out.println(gpas[9001]);
```

When you run the program you should see an output similar to the following:

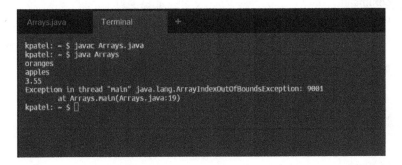

Figure 5.2: Using an index that is out of range results in an exception.

Declaring Empty Arrays

All of the arrays we've filled so far, have been filled manually. We've then printed them by calling indexes individually. We don't have to do this. The declaration and instantiation (fancy word for creation) of an array can be done with no values so long as you know how many elements you plan on putting inside of your array.

Here is an example of how to do so:

```
int[] vals = new int[10];
```

In this case, we are creating an integer array with 10 slots. The slots are currently filled with integers containing the value zero, as zero is the default value for an integer without an explicitly assigned value.

Rather than putting a series of values after the declaration statement, we commanded the JVM to make a new empty array with enough space for ten integer type numbers.

Remember, Java is zero-indexed so the last slot in this array isn't called by putting a ten in the brackets. ten is simply the number of elements within the array. The last element is referenced with a nine.

```
vals[9];
```

The above will access the last slot of the array. The first slot is accessed by placing a 0 in the brackets.

The technical term for the way *arrays count* is "zero-based". (Java is zero-indexed. Arrays are zero-based).

Editing Array Members

You can also use the index of an array member to change the values of different members in the list. This is done with an assignment statement as in assigning a value to a standard variable. The following statement will change the zeroth index of the GPA list:

gpas[0] = 4.0

Note that the indexes of the other members of the array are not affected.

This is also one way that we can fill our empty arrays. We would simply reassign an empty slot to a value we would like.

Sorting Arrays

We've manipulated and stored a lot of data so far. We have not, however, organized much data.

Arrays are a powerful organizational tool. One reason is because of the **sort()** method. It does exactly what it sounds like—it sorts the members of the array. The sort method is called a bit differently from normal methods though. Sort() is called as a static member of the array class like this:

Arrays.sort(<Array>);

Make a new file and copy this code. My file is called ArraySortDemo.java:

```
import java.util.Arrays;

public class ArraySortDemo{

  public static void main (String[] args) {
```

```java
String[] groceries = {
    "oranges","apples","milk","bread","butter","pepper",
"salt","sugar","pears"
    };

System.out.println("___UNSORTED ARRAY___");

for(String a:groceries){
   System.out.print(a + " ");
}
System.out.println();
System.out.println("___SORTED ARRAY___");

Arrays.sort(groceries);

for(String a:groceries){
   System.out.print(a + " ");
}

System.out.println();

  }


}
```

Note: Don't worry if you don't understand the for loops. They're used to print our array. We'll cover them in the next section.

Run your program with the Java command. Your output should look something like this:

```
kpatel: ~ $ javac ArraySortDemo.java
kpatel: ~ $ java ArraySortDemo
___UNSORTED ARRAY___
oranges apples milk bread butter pepper salt sugar pears
___SORTED ARRAY___
apples bread butter milk oranges pears pepper salt sugar
kpatel: ~ $ []
```

Figure 5.3: After the **sort()** function runs, the groceries list is reindexed. It's now in alphabetical order!

The sort method will also order numbers from smallest to largest, and organize other primitive data.

Printing Arrays

So far the only way we've been printing information from arrays is through referencing an individual array element. But what if we need to print out a whole array?

Copy this file below:

```
public class PrintingArrays{

  public static void main (String[] args) {

    int[] oneToTen = {
      1,2,3,4,5,6,7,8,9,10
```

```
    };

        System.out.println(oneToTen);

    }

}
```

Executing the code above results in non-readable text:

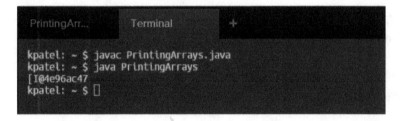

Figure 5.4: Passing the variable name printed an internal reference used by the Java compiler. Odd.

Instead, we have to use a loop. There are several ways to do this; I'm going to show you the two easiest and most frequently used.

With a for loop

The first method uses a simple for loop to print out the array. Replace the print method with these few of code in PrintingArrays:

```
for(int x = 0; x<oneToTen.length; x++){
          System.out.println(oneToTen[x]);
      }
```

Now if you run your program you'll see that the contents of your array have been printed:

Figure 5.5: Awesome! We printed the array.

The way this loop works is very simple. The local variable we create to track the number of times our loop has iterated is used as the index value when we call an array element. As a result after iteration, the value of the variable increases by one and the slot we're referencing changes.

In other words: x starts as zero. The next iteration changes x's value from zero to one. Due to the square brackets containing the dynamic variable x rather than a static number the index that we are calling, which was originally index zero, switches to index one.

The number of iterations is set using the **.length** property which returns the total number of elements in our array.

With a for-each loop

The second method of printing is through the use of a modified for loop called a for-each loop. The syntax for this loop is simpler than that of the regular for loop.

Add the following code to the end of your PrintingArrays program:

```
System.out.println("_____With a for each loop_____");

    for(int print:oneToTen){
        System.out.println(print);
    }
```

The first line in this snippet of code prints a separator, so we know which loop is generating the output.

Next is the for-each loop. The statement within the for loop's parentheses is shorter, consisting of two components rather than three. This statement also fails to conform to what we've learned about traditional for loops, as it lacks an iterator and conditional. This different statement is what makes this a for-each loop rather than a regular for loop. Whatever code is put inside the loop will be performed **for each** member of the array.

In this case we're printing the array.

The statement within the parentheses of the loop consists of a variable declaration, whose type must match the type of the array you intended to call the loop on and the name of the array you intend to use the loop on.

If you, for example, wanted to print our grocery list array, the for-each loop would look like this:

```
for(String item: groceries){
          System.out.println(item);
      }
```

Because groceries is an array of strings, the variable 'item' is a string as well.

This needs to be true for all variables and datatypes declared for use in a for-each loop. If you intend to print an array of integers, the holder variable that is declared within the parentheses must have a type of integer.

Arrays are objects and you can use a number of methods associated with the Array object. You might want to take a look at the official Java documentation and see the functions that you can use with arrays. The documentation is available at
http://docs.oracle.com/Javase/7/docs/api/Java/util/Arrays.html.

Remember: Learning how to read documentation is a valuable skill.

ArrayLists

Arrays are very useful, but they are also rather limited in what they can do. An example is the array's inability to be expanded after instantiation. If I have an array with ten elements I can't add an eleventh element to the end of the array. With ArrayLists we gain new functionality and the ability to add different types of objects into one data structure, but that isn't done often.

At this point you may be wondering why we bother with arrays at all if we have ArrayLists. The answer is efficiency. ArrayLists take up more memory than arrays. In bigger programs this means they can cause it to run slower than if we just used arrays.

ArrayLists, just like Scanners, are reference or class type objects. Their declaration looks like this:

ArrayList **name** = new ArrayList();

It should be noted that ArrayLists cannot be filled upon initialization like arrays. The only way to fill them is through the **.add()** method. You should also be aware that unless you put an integer in the parenthesis of the ArrayList's constructor it will be made with a default size of ten slots.

If your ArrayList is full the **.add()** method will simply add a new member and append what you placed in the parenthesis to the end of the list.

Now let's try an example. I put mine in a file called ArrayLists:

```java
import java.util.*;

public class ArrayLists{

  public static void main (String[] args) {

    ArrayList languages = new ArrayList(3);
    languages.add("Spanish");
    languages.add("French");
    languages.add("English");

    System.out.println(languages.size());

    languages.add("German");

    System.out.println(languages.size());
  }

}
```

The first line in the main method declares a new ArrayList that we named languages and gave it a size of three.

Talk the Talk: There are several ways to say you used a method. The most common terms are 'call' or 'invoke'. When I programmer says 'I invoked the method' he or she is really saying they used the method.

The next three lines of code invoke the add method to fill up the ArrayList. Then the size method is called to see how large the ArrayList is. After that one more element is appended to the end of the ArrayList, increasing the size from the original three slots to four.

When you run the code, your output should appear something like this:

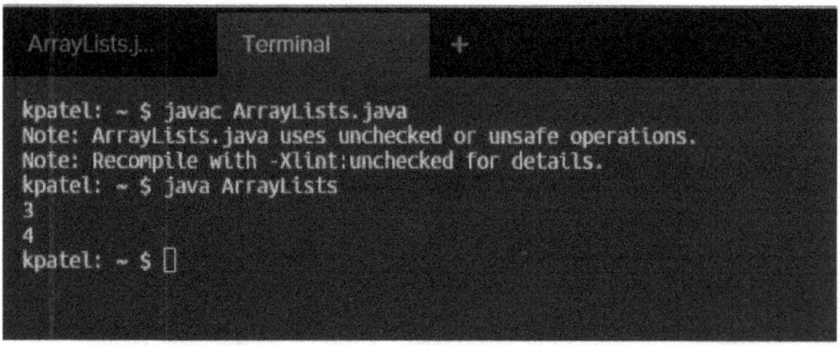

Figure 5.6: We can see how the size of our ArrayList increased when we added an element to the end.

Java printed two notes in addition to the output of the program. This occured because we are using an unparameterized ArrayList. An unperamiterized ArrayList is an ArrayList that's type hasn't been specified. As a result variables of different types can be stored within the same ArrayList and cause exceptions due to type mismatches.

To alleviate this issue, we have to type our list to take one specific object like arrays do. Rather than a standard declaration and instantiation, we add a slight modification to each part so it looks like this:

ArrayList<DataType> name = new ArrayList<DataType>();

Talk the Talk: An unparamaterized ArrayList accepts what's known as a generic type. A generic type is a type that can be specified later by the programmer in order to improve functionality. The type can be anything, including custom classes that you implement and design yourself.

Let's modify the code in our ArrayLists.java file to follow this practice:

```java
import java.util.*;

public class ArrayLists{

    public static void main (String[] args) {

        ArrayList<String> languages = new
ArrayList<String>(3);
        languages.add("Spanish");
        languages.add("French");
        languages.add("English");

        System.out.println(languages.size());

        languages.add("German");

        System.out.println(languages.size());
    }
}
```

Now when we recompile and run our code, there's no problem!

```
kpatel: ~ $ javac ArrayLists.java
Note: ArrayLists.java uses unchecked or unsafe operations.
Note: Recompile with -Xlint:unchecked for details.
kpatel: ~ $ java ArrayLists
3
4
kpatel: ~ $ javac ArrayLists.java
kpatel: ~ $ java ArrayLists
3
4
kpatel: ~ $ 
```

Figure 5.7: Much better. Typing our ArrayList got rid of that pesky warning.

Now the final thing to know about ArrayLists is how to obtain data from them. Unlike arrays, we don't reference by indexes. Instead, we use a method to retrieve the data: The **.get(#)** method. The number in the parentheses is the index value of the element you want to access. Just like Arrays, ArrayLists are zero-based.

Add the following line to your code, recompile and run to see it in action:

System.out.println(languages.get(0));

When you recompile and run, the output should look something like this:

Figure 5.8: We got then printed the first element of our ArrayList.

There are a number of other methods for ArrayLists that are rather useful. The most notable being the **.set()** method, which replaces values much like reassigning with arrays.

The official documentation is located here:

http://docs.oracle.com/Javase/7/docs/api/Java/util/ArrayList.html

Immutables

Immutables are very similar to ArrayLists with one important exception: Immutables are non-dynamic. This means once an Immutable is defined the values within it cannot be changed. Let's start a new program where we will define an Immutable.

Copy this code into a file named ImmutablesDemo.java:

```java
import java.util.*;

public class ImmutablesDemo{

    public static void main (String[] args) {

        //Note: Arrays cannot be made immutable. So instead,
we use Lists.
        String[] turn = {"600", "800", "1024", "1280", "1366",
"1920"};
        List<String> list = Java.util.Arrays.asList(turn);
        List<String> unmodList =
Collections.unmodifiableList(list);


        for(String p: unmodList){
            System.out.println(p);
        }
        System.out.println();
        System.out.print(unmodList.get(0));


        unmodList.add("464");
        }


    }
```

Compile the code then run it using the Java command and carefully examine the output.

```
Immutable...        Terminal            +

kpatel: ~ $ javac ImmutablesDemo.java
kpatel: ~ $ java ImmutablesDemo
600
800
1024
1280
1366
1920

600Exception in thread "main" java.lang.UnsupportedOperationException
        at java.util.Collections$UnmodifiableCollection.add(Collections.java:1075)
        at ImmutablesDemo.main(ImmutablesDemo.java:19)
kpatel: ~ $ []
```

Figure 5.9: Note that we're able to access the complete immutable, a single index within the immutable, but when reassigning a value within an immutable, an error is generated. An immutable is non-dynamic and once initiated, the values within it cannot be changed.

Immutable are for storing data that does not change over the life of a program. For example, in the program above, the screen widths are unlikely to change.

HashTables

HashTables are yet another data structure. They are perfect for storing paired data, sometimes known as *key: value* data. In this type of data, instead of a numerical index, each data point is indexed by a key which is determined by the programmer. State names and state capitals or towns and zip codes are both examples of where HashTables can be useful for storing data.

Seasoned programmers may find HashTables to be very similar to Dictionaries. This is because HashTables were derived from them. (Dictionaries are the parent class of Hashtables)

Consider the following program:

```java
import java.util.*;
public class HashTabs{

    public static void main (String[] args) {

    Hashtable <String,String> statesAndCapitols = new
Hashtable<String,String>();


        statesAndCapitols.put("Connecticut","Hartford");
        statesAndCapitols.put("New York","Albany");
        statesAndCapitols.put("Mississippi","Jackson");
        statesAndCapitols.put("Maine","Augusta");
        statesAndCapitols.put("Montana","Helena");
        statesAndCapitols.put("Texas","Austin");

        String ConnCap = statesAndCapitols.get("Connecticut");

        System.out.println(ConnCap);



    }
```

```
        }
```

When you run the program with the Java command you'll see the output "Hartford". This is the result of the key (or index) for "Hartford" being "Connecticut." Note the print command and how it is used to access the value in the HashTable.

Just like arrays, Java's HashTables are an object and have functions that can be associated with them. Let's take a look at one of these functions. Update your code so it appears like this:

```
port java.util.*;
public class HashTabs{

    public static void main (String[] args) {

    Hashtable <String,String> statesAndCapitols = new
Hashtable<String,String>();


        statesAndCapitols.put("Connecticut","Hartford");
        statesAndCapitols.put("New York","Albany");
        statesAndCapitols.put("Mississippi","Jackson");
        statesAndCapitols.put("Maine","Augusta");
        statesAndCapitols.put("Montana","Helena");
        statesAndCapitols.put("Texas","Austin");
```

```
        String ConnCap = statesAndCapitols.get("Connecticut");

        System.out.println(ConnCap);

        System.out.println("Values: " +
statesAndCapitols.values());
        System.out.println("Keys: " +
statesAndCapitols.keySet());

    }

}
```

Run your code on the command line using the Java command. Your result should appear similar to figure 5.10:

```
Terminal    ▾ ×    +

kpatel: ~ $ javac HashTabs.java
kpatel: ~ $ java HashTabs
Hartford
Values: [Helena, Augusta, Hartford, Albany, Austin, Jackson]
Keys: [Montana, Maine, Connecticut, New York, Texas, Mississippi]
kpatel: ~ $ █
```

Figure 5.10: Output demonstrating two of the functions used with dictionaries—**values()** and **keySet()**

You'll note that the **values()** function returns all of the values in the dictionary, while the **keySet()** function returns all of the keys.

This short chapter can only give you a broad introduction to working with data in programming. Almost every program, to some degree, works with data. Being effective at working with data is an important part of any programmer's toolbox.

Chapter 6:
Putting It All Together

Classes and objects represent not just a programming concept, but a way of looking at the world and solving problems. Classes and objects, at a high level, represent a process of classification—an activity that is as old as science. When we create a class, we create a model of an object that breaks the object down to its core activities and attributes. Java is an Object Oriented language, meaning that it is completely dependent on the Class and Object structure and everything must be contained in one. Java isn't the only language that supports objects. It's good to have an understanding of objects as they are a very common occurrence in programming.

Class Versus Objects

I often tell my students to think of a class as a blueprint of an object. From that blueprint, many instances of the class (objects) can be created. Think of planned housing communities: a single blueprint may be used to build many different homes. These homes may vary in substantial ways—they may be different colors, have different kitchen counters, and different fixtures in the bathrooms—but they are all still based on the same blueprint.

In programming, a class defines how an object of the class is described and what it can do. It might be useful to think of classes as a set of adjectives and a set of verbs. The adjectives give us a way to describe the class, while the verbs tell us what the class can do. The set of adjectives used to describe a class are known as fields. The set of verbs associated with a class are known as methods.

If we were describing a class "vehicle" we might include the following methods and properties:

Fields (Adjectives)	**Methods** (Verbs)
color	accelerate()
weight	decelerate()
he height	turnLeft()
topSpeed	turnRight()
vehicleType	startIgnition()
	stopIgnition()

Obviously this model is greatly simplified. If we were truly trying to represent a vehicle in code, we'd likely have to use several interrelated classes. In Java we also have to declare the type of data each property would hold. For example, the color property would hold a string, while weight, height and top speed could be integers. When we create an instance of the Vehicle Class that we defined in the previous table, we might assign a value to all of the properties, like this:

```
String color = "blue";
double weight = 5565.3;
int height = 48;
int topSpeed = 90;
```

String vehicleType = "car";

This example assumes an instance (object) created called theVehicle.

Coding a Class in Java

Let's write the code that represents an Animal class in Java. We'll also create an instance of that class called myDog in another file, a bit later.

```java
public class Animal{

    private static int numberOfAnimals = 0;
    public int length;
    public String color;
    public double weight;
    public boolean hasFur;

    public Animal(int Length, double Weight, String Color,
boolean Fur){

        color = Color;
        weight = Weight;
        hasFur = Fur;
        length = Length;
        numberOfAnimals ++;
    }
```

There are definitely a few new things here. The first is that we don't have a public static void main. This is because this program doesn't run in the way that we've been seeing so far. The main method is generally the entrance point for the JVM to start executing our code. It will be in our driver class, which we'll write later. We start our definition of the class with the **public class** keywords and then the name of the class—in this case, "Animal." The public keyword gives information about visibility. It tells the JVM that any class is allowed to make objects from this class and call its methods. The Class keyword informs Java as to what this file is. Next, you'll notice I declare a variable called **numOfAnimals** and initialize it at zero. The numOfAnimals variable is designed to do some internal housekeeping in the class. Its job, specifically, is to track how many instances of Animal we create. The static keyword between the datatype and the visibility level (which in this case is private) is what enables us to use this variable as a tracker. Static means that you don't have to create an instance of a class in order to access or modify this information. This means that each object doesn't have an instance of "numOfAnimals" rather it exists in the class.

After numOfAnimals I simply create a number of variables detailing information about our animal: things such as weight, color, length and if it has fur or not.

A keyword is a reserved word that cannot be used for anything other than its intended functions. Examples include: public, private, for, while and do. Generally keywords will be highlighted by your text editor. The editor I'm using on Koding colors them purple, as seen on the left side of figure 6.1. Keywords cannot be used as variable, function or class names, due to the fact that they're already reserved.

We then define with the **public** keyword in the Animal file what's known as a "constructor". This method is very important. It does three things: details the information that we need in order to make an object based on this class, preforms any internal housekeeping and assigns initial values to the fields. It will be executed every time that an object is created based on of your class.

The constructor is called by the driver class below.

I named mine AnimalDriver.java:

```
public class AnimalDriver{

    public static void main (String[] args) {

        Animal myDog = new Animal(19, 12, "brown", "true");

    }

}
```

The particular instance of Animal that we are creating, called **myDog**, has a length of 19, weight of 12, is brown and has fur. The first four lines of constructor assign these values that are passed into the instance. You may be wondering how we determined the order of the information to put into the class. The answer is pretty simple; the constructor accepts arguments in the order that the class's constructor is coded. In our class, the order of the data types was: int, double, String and Boolean. This means when we call the constructor, that's the order that arguments must follow.

Figure 6.1: Creating the class (left) and driver class(right) in Koding

Examine the following line:

numOfAnimals++;

This line is designed to increment the value of numOfAnimals, the internal housekeeping variable that keeps track of how many instances of Animal that we generate. The actual instance is generated with the code in the driver class which can be seen here in a file called AnimalDriver.java:

```java
public class AnimalDriver{

    public static void main (String[] args) {

        Animal myDog = new Animal(19, 12, "brown", "true");

    }

}
```

Adding Some Methods

Let's change up and add to our initial code:

```java
public class Animal{

    private static int numberOfAnimals = 0;
    public int length;
```

```java
    public String color;
    public double weight;
    public boolean hasFur;
    public boolean isHungry;

    public Animal(int Length, double Weight, String Color,
boolean Fur, boolean Hungry){

        color = Color;
        weight = Weight;
        hasFur = Fur;
        isHungry = Hungry;
        length = Length;
        numberOfAnimals ++;
    }

    public String walk(){
        return "Animal is walking";
    }

    public String eat(){

        isHungry = false;
        weight += .1;
        return "Animal has eaten.\n" + "Animal now weighs: " +
weight + " pounds";

    }

    public String getLength(){
        return "Animal's length is " + length;
    }

    }
```

Now that we've added to our animal class, we need to add to the driver class in order to continue testing.

Rewrite the code in your AnimalDriver file so it looks like this, then recompile and run it.

```
public class AnimalDriver{

    public static void main (String[] args) {

        Animal myDog = new Animal(19, 12, "brown", true);


        System.out.println(myDog.walk());
        System.out.println(myDog.eat());

        System.out.println(myDog.getLength());

    }

}
```

When you run the code with the Java command, the result should appear something like this:

Figure 6.2: Creating an instance of a class and manipulating it

You'll notice that I've added an additional property, with the datatype Boolean to the class: hungry. This property is designed simply to track whether or not the instance of Animal is hungry. When we create the instance of Animal called myDog, we set the value of the hungry property to true.

We've also added two methods to our class. The first method, walk(), simply prints out the message "Animal is walking."

The second method, eat(), is more complex. It interacts with the properties of the object. First, the eat() method sets the value of the hungry property to "false." It then informs the user that the Animal is eating via the print statement. Finally, because the animal is eating, we access the weight property and add .1 to its value.

After the class definition and the instantiation of the myDog instance, we run the walk() and eat() methods.

You'll notice that all of these methods use the return keyword.

The definition of these methods contains what's known as a "return type". It appears in the declaration of the method after the visibility level. This is the reason the Scanner object needs several methods to take input from the prompt; methods can only return one datatype & one object. In all of our instances, we're returning a string. When we call the methods in our AnimalDriver class, whatever the method returns to us will be a string. This means we can set a String to capture the return value of our method in a variable:

public String walkText = myDog.walk();

Note that while we have so far returned primitive types like int, float or boolean, we can also return reference types such as ArrayLists.

The **return** keyword itself does two things.

The first thing is send back to the method call whatever you put on the rest of the line. If you put an expression, it sends back the result. If you put a string it sends back the whole string.

The next thing the return keyword does is marks the completion of the method. As soon as your method returns something it will exit regardless of what is after the return in the code. This is useful because you could place the return statement within an if statement and have it end pre-maturely under set criteria.

Some methods don't have to return anything. An example that we've encountered is print method. In this case the return type is "void", which goes in place of the data type. An example of a method with this kind of declaration is as follows.

public void **name**(<Datatype>Parameter){}

It should be noted that the return keyword can be used to force a void method to exit as well. Simply type "return", and a semicolon to end the line, and stop the execution of the method.

Multiple Instances
You'll remember from our initial discussion that a class is merely a blueprint and multiple objects can be constructed from that class. Enter this revised code in your text editor:

```java
public class Animal{

    private static int numberOfAnimals = 0;
    public String name;
    public int length;
    public String color;
    public double weight;
    public boolean hasFur;
    public boolean isHungry;

    public Animal(String Name, String Color, int Length,
double Weight, boolean Fur, boolean Hungry){

        color = Color;
        weight = Weight;
        hasFur = Fur;
        isHungry = Hungry;
        length = Length;
        name = Name;
    }

    public String walk(){
        return name +" is walking";
    }
```

```java
    public String eat(){

        isHungry = false;
        weight += .1;
        return name + " has eaten.\n" + name + "  now weighs: "
+ weight + " pounds";

    }

    public String getLength(){
        return name + "'s length is " + length;
    }


}
```

I've added yet another property to the Animal class. The name property is designed to hold the name of the Animal instance. Keep in mind; this is distinct from the name of the code reference to the instance.

Now let's update our Animal Driver class to reflect the new functionality.
Copy this revised code:

```java
    public class AnimalDriver{

        public static void main (String[] args) {

            Animal myDog = new Animal("Sparky","Grey", 17,
56.4, true, true);
            Animal yourDog = new Animal("Rover","Brown", 19,
41.8, true, true);
```

```
        System.out.println(myDog.walk());
        System.out.println(myDog.eat());

        System.out.println(yourDog.walk());
        System.out.println(yourDog.eat());

        System.out.println(yourDog.getLength());

    }

}
```

The original Animal instance myDog has a value of "Sparky" in the name property, while the new object has a value of "Rover" in the name property.

Running the new code should result in output similar to the following:

Figure 6.3: Two instances of Animal objects are created—Sparky and Rover.

Extending Classes

The object oriented structure does more than allow us to simply represent objects as code in one file. It allows us to build an entire hierarchy of objects to represent our real life problem space. Let's take another look at Vehicles.

In the world we have numerous types of vehicles. Some work on the ground, some work in the water and others in the air. To properly represent a vehicle in an object oriented manner, we need to determine what they all have in common. All vehicles have a top speed, a weight and a color. All vehicles are either moving, or still.

As a result we can create a new object that contains all of these common attributes, so we don't have to code them each time we want to create a variant of a vehicle.

Copy the following code, and save it as **Vehicle.java**:

```java
public class Vehicle{

    int topSpeed;
    String color;
    double weight;
    boolean isMoving;

    public Vehicle(int setSpeed, String setColor, double setWeight, boolean tellIfMoving){

        topSpeed = setSpeed;
        color = setColor;
        weight = setWeight;
        isMoving = tellIfMoving;

    }

```

```
    public boolean startMoving(){

        isMoving = true;
        return "Vehicle is moving.";
    }

    public boolean stopMoving(){

        isMoving = false;
        return "Vehicle isn't moving.";
    }


}
```

The code above summarizes the basic attribute of vehicles. But if we need to represent a car, there is information we need that wouldn't be relevant if we were representing a boat. But we would still need all of the attributes described in the Vehicle class. Does this mean we copy all of this code into two different files in just to represent these types of vehicles? We could, but that would be inefficient. Instead we *extend* the vehicle class.

By extending the vehicle class, we create what is known as a **child class**. The child class inherits the fields, methods and even the constructor of the parent (Vehicle in our case) class.

Open up a new file in your text editor, and save the following code as **GroundVehicle.java**:

```java
public class GroundVehicle extends Vehicle{


    int numWheels;
    String vehicleType;

    public GroundVehicle(int setSpeed, String setColor,
double setWeight,                    boolean tellIfMoving, int
setNumWheels,String type){
        super(setSpeed, setColor, setWeight, tellIfMoving);
        numWheels = setNumWheels;
        vehicleType = type;
    }

    public String startMoving(){

       isMoving = true;
       return vehicleType + " is driving";

    }
    public String stopMoving(){
       isMoving = false;
       return vehicleType + " isn't driving";
    }
    public String whatColor(){
       return color;
    }


}
```

The first line of this code is slightly different from what you're used to
from this chapter. There is the addition of the "extends" keyword

followed by Vehicle. This notifies Java that GroundVehicle is a child of Vehicle. In other words GroundVehicle is derived from Vehicle.

In Java, all classes, regardless of if they contain the extends keyword, are an extension of the Object class. As a result at the top of every hierarchal tree sits the Object class.

Our tree appears as follows:
GroundVehicle is a Vehicle which is an Object.

Talk the Talk: In object oriented programming when a programmer references the parent of a child they say the child class shares an "is a/an" relationship with the parent class.

The next lines of the code add two new fields to our object. numWheels contains the number of wheels our GroundVehicle object has. The vehicleType variable allows us to pass in a string like "car", "motorcycle" or "truck". Both of these new variables exist in addition to all of the variables in the Vehicle class. Vehicle's variables can be accessed through the "super" keyword. Since GroundVehicle is a subclass of Vehicle, GroundVehicle has inherited Vehicle's attributes and functionality.

The super keyword allows you to reference fields, constructors and methods of the direct parent (class after the "extends" keyword) class.

We already referenced the constructor by using the super keyword in the constructor of our GroundVehicle class. We treated the super keyword like the instantiation statement of Vehicle.

The normal instantiation would look like this:

new Vehicle(100,"Orange",1034.2, false);

"new Vehicle" has been replaced by "super" within the constructor and as a result all of the hidden fields within GroundVehicle will be populated upon construction due to us invoking the parent class's constructor.

After the constructor we have three methods. They change one variable within the vehicle class and then return a string that confirms their change. Read the name of the first two methods in GroundVehicle and then the first two methods in Vehicle. When methods in a child class share the same name as methods in their superclass, they override the superclass method. We are changing the functionality of the method and nothing more. If we changed anything more, such as the return type, we would be overloading the method.

Remember, we need a driver class in order to use our objects.

Copy the following code into a file named **VehicleDriver.java**:

```java
public class VehicleDriver{

    public static void main(String[] args){

        Vehicle transportationMachine = new
Vehicle(50,"Blue",210,false);

        System.out.println(transportationMachine.startMoving());

    }

}
```

The resulting output of this code is:

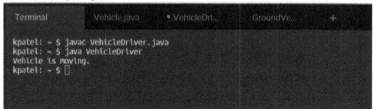

Figure 6.4: The output is the string we typed in the Vehicle Driver class, as that is what we put after the return statement.

Let's add some additional code to our VehicleDriver to get a better idea of what's going on. Add this code into your Vehicle Driver class:

```java
GroundVehicle horseAndBuggy = new GroundVehicle(5, "Black", 300, false, 4,"Horse and Buggy");

String result = horseAndBuggy.startMoving();
System.out.println(result);
```

Once we recompile and run the output looks something like this:

Figure 6.5: The more specific method in our GroundVehicle class resulted in a more specific output.

The first line of this code snippet is the instantiation for the GroundVehicle object which we use to make a horse and buggy. The next line makes a string, and sets it to the output of the startMoving method. The final line prints result.

Finally let's look at one more thing that class extensions are capable of.

Copy these last few lines into the driver class:
```
Vehicle goKart = new GroundVehicle(25,"Yellow", 3, true, 4, "GoKart" );

System.out.println(goKart.startMoving());
```

Look at the declaration and instantiation of the object. They do not match. However when we compile and run this code, there are no issues due to the fact that GroundVehicle is a type of Vehicle. Since the GroundVehicle class is derived from the Vehicle class, a Vehicle type variable can be used to hold a GroundVehicle type object, like we've done in our code.

However a GroundVehicle type variable **cannot** be used to hold a Vehicle type object! A GroundVehicle is a Vehicle, but a Vehicle is not necessarily a GroundVehicle. GroundVehicle has parameters that not all Vehicles have, an example being number of wheels.

This is true in all programming trees. The less vague objects can be contained within more vague variables. Vaguer objects however cannot be contained within a more specific variable.

This also means that you can place a GroundVehicle, or a Vehicle within an Object type variable, as all reference type objects are derived from the Object class. (Everything is an object.)

At this point you may be wondering what happens when you call the "startMoving" method on the next line. Will it use the more specific method within the GroundVehicle class or the vague method within the Vehicle class?

Well if you compile and run the code, the result looks like this:

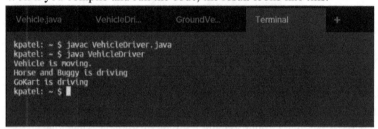

Figure 6.6: It used the more specific method!

Despite the variable being of the Vehicle type, the object that the variable referenced was of the type GroundVehicle. Due to the object being of the Ground Vehicle type, when we called the method on the object it did what it was supposed to do and executed the code that it had access to: The more specific method.

I encourage you to add code and experiment with the vehicle class, or make your own classes and methods to see what you can do.

A good project would be to represent some other real system in code. This section was designed to give you only a basic introduction to object-oriented programming with classes and objects. However, you will find that these foundational concepts can be applied to many modern programming languages.

The end of this section also brings us to the conclusion of this book. You now know the foundations of programming using the Java programming language. You will find this information useful whether you continue your study in Java, or move to other areas of development, such as web applications or mobile.

Whatever direction you go, I wish you the best of luck.

Online Courses from LearnToProgram

Become a Certified Web Developer Level One

Become a Certified Web Developer Level Two

Certified Mobile Developer

Roadmap to Web Developer

HTML and CSS for Beginners (with HTML5

Javascript for Beginners

Programming for Absolute Beginners

PHP and MySQL for Beginners

jQuery for Beginners

CSS Development with CSS3

Node.js for Beginners

Advanced Javascript Development

AJAX Development

SQL Database for Beginners

Ruby on Rails for Beginners

Famo.us Javascript Framework

GitHub Fundamentals

Creating a PHP Login Script

Front End Developer with Adobe Dreamweaver

Codeless Web Development with Adobe Muse

Mobile App Development with HTML5

10 Apps in 10 Weeks

Java Programming for Beginners

Swift Language Fundamentals

iOS Development for Beginners

Android Development for Beginners

10 Apps in 10 Weeks:iOS Edition

Python for Beginners

Construct 2 for Beginners

Game Development with Unity

Mobile Game Development for iOS

3D Fundamentals with iOS

Project Management using Microsoft Project

.Net for Beginners

C++ for Beginners